WILDSAM

Southwest Art

PHOTO ALMANAC

ISBN 978-1-4671-9973-5

Editor	Rebecca Worby
Photo Editor	John McCauley
Illustrator	Gabriella Trujillo
Designer	Alan Kahler
Managing Editor	Zach Dundas

Founder & Editor in Chief	Taylor Bruce

Featuring	Tony Abeyta
	Keri Ataumbi
	Patrociño Barela
	Maynard Dixon
	R.C. Gorman
	Maria Martinez
	Nampeyo
	Georgia O'Keeffe
	Virgil Ortiz
	Fritz Scholder
	Jaune Quick-to-See Smith
	Roxanne Swentzell
	Doug West
	Beatien Yazz
	and more

To learn more about Wildsam,
visit www.wildsam.com

CONTENTS

Introduction

The quality of the light. The landscape's color palette—much more varied and vibrant than the word "desert" implies—and the way that the light itself changes those colors so that the land itself is never the same twice. The sky that spreads wide like an offering. All these contribute to the ineffable pull of the American Southwest. It is a region that lends itself to the creation of beautiful things. It demands a kind of reverence, and for many, that reverence translates into artmaking. Across many centuries, for Indigenous peoples of the region, creation often sprang from necessity—the black-on-black pottery of Maria Martinez and her family in San Ildefonso Pueblo was always stunning, but it only became "art," and earned international renown, when the fine art world embraced it. Today, though Georgia O'Keeffe may be the most famous artist associated with the region, the list of those for whom the Southwest taps into something generative and profound is ever-growing. From trail-blazers like Fritz Scholder and R.C. Gorman to contemporary forces like Tony Abeyta, Roxanne Swentzell and Virgil Ortiz, it would take several volumes much larger than this one to illuminate them all. What unifies these artists, whether they make paintings or pots, sculpture or jewelry, whether they are indigenous to this place or arrived as curious strangers— is that their work could come from nowhere else.

1

In the Southwest, inspiration is rooted in the vast and varied land

Landscape

DOUG WEST
Heading Home
Oil on canvas
2016

EMMANUEL MONZON
From the *Urban Sprawl: Emptiness* series
*In Monzon's Urban Sprawl photos, the mundanity
of human-made structures contrasts starkly with
vast landscapes.*

BY
KYLE
PAOLETTA

Dispatch: DESERT PHOTOGRAPHY

In Timothy O'Sullivan's 1873 photograph of Canyon de Chelly, there are three tents pitched on the valley floor that would be completely invisible were the white of their canvas not so bright. Too small to fully assert the presence of humanity in this overpowering natural space, the tents' purpose in the image is merely to provide a sense of scale, to underscore the immensity of the featured trio of sandstone pinnacles that soar 1,200 feet into the sepia sky. • O'Sullivan is remembered as the Southwest's first landscape photographer, but his decision to prioritize topography over people was not a matter of artistic whimsy: he journeyed to the region from New York to contribute to a series of geological surveys that would determine the best railroad routes and allow the region to be more efficiently colonized. His images helped create the myth of the desert as an empty expanse, a place in need of filling. • When Ansel Adams arrived at Canyon de Chelly a half century later, he traded O'Sullivan's valley-floor perspective for a high vantage, directing his camera down into the canyon to highlight the sweeping S-curve of a dry riverbed; at White Sands, in New Mexico, Adams shot when the blinding sun was low on the horizon, allowing him to transfigure a sweeping sand dune into a wave of rippling shadow. Esther Henderson's vivid photographs in the '60s exchanged Adams' striking architectural forms for the little moments of spontaneous life glimpsed amid the austerity, like pink wildflowers climbing sand dunes or a "golden pocket" of yellow-leafed cottonwoods growing in an arroyo's cradle. • Rather than depict the Southwest as untrammeled, some contemporary photographers have taken bold steps to highlight the infrastructure that has overspread the desert since O'Sullivan's day. By doing so, they've recentered humanity in the region and complicated the old notion of it as a virgin wilderness. Emmanuel Monzon's series *Urban Sprawl: Emptiness* includes an image of a wide, white plain seemingly dominated by a picnic table and a trash can. Victoria Sambunaris' work is subtler but operates in a similar vein. One photograph appears at first to merely capture a red-rock mesa reflected in an expanse of crystal-clear water. But this pond isn't natural. It's an evaporation pool used to mine for potassium chloride [better known as potash] at a facility near Moab, Utah. Through Sambunaris' lens, differentiating between natural environment and despoiling civilization becomes nearly impossible. • By foregrounding the roads, power plants and mines that branch farther across the region every year, artists like Monzon and Sambunaris speak profoundly to the often befuddling reality of the 21st-century Southwest. To look out beyond a newly platted subdivision at a vista of mesas thrust out of the bare earth by tectonic happenstance forces a paradoxical consideration of both the presumption inherent in attempting to bring this landscape to heel and the acknowledgment that the desert has never really been empty. Be it in McMansions, tents or cliff dwellings dating back millennia, human beings have always called the Southwest home—for better and for worse. So much is lost by tilting the viewfinder up until those vexing ribbons of asphalt disappear entirely.

"I wish you could see what I see out the
window—the earth pink and yellow
cliffs to the north—the full pale moon about
to go down in an early morning lavender
sky behind a very long beautiful tree-covered
mesa to the west—pink and purple hills in
front and the scrubby fine dull green
cedars—and a feeling of much space—
It is a very beautiful world."

Georgia O'Keeffe
1942 letter to the painter Arthur Dove

Tony Vaccaro, Courtesy of Tony Vaccaro Studio

Tony Abeyta

For Tony Abeyta, art is
an expression of life
experiences. His work
is an ongoing effort to
explore what he's seen,
heard, felt—and what
it all means.

Navajo artist Tony Abeyta is inspired by natural rhythms. That is the constant across his decades of mixed media and oil paintings, whose subject matter ranges from Native American iconography to modernist landscapes. In 2012, he received the New Mexico Governor's Award for Excellence in the Arts. Several prestigious museums feature Abeyta's works, including the Smithsonian's National Museum of the American Indian, the Autry Museum of the American West in Los Angeles and the Heard Museum in Phoenix. Raised in Gallup, Abeyta splits his time between Santa Fe and Berkeley, California.

ON CHILDHOOD IN GALLUP

I didn't really want to do art when I was a kid. I grew up in a small town. There was one gallery there, and it sold predominantly traditional American Indian stuff. I didn't come out of that school. So I was looking for other things that I could focus on. I thought maybe I could be an architect or something. My mom did weaving and ceramics. My dad was a painter who came out of the Santa Fe Indian School in the '30s, but he struggled. He had a full-time job. So art didn't look sustainable as I was growing up.

ON FINDING A PATH

Throughout my teen years, I worked at movie theaters as a union projectionist, but I grew pretty frustrated with that job. I decided to go to art school at the recommendation of my sister Elizabeth. She had gone to the Institute of American Indian Arts in Santa Fe and said that I should apply. When I got to IAIA, I was exposed to the possibility that maybe I could be an artist. There were a number of mainstream galleries that were representing American Indians as artists. I saw a show that was a survey of contemporary American Indian artists like Fritz Scholder and Harry Fonseca—most of them being from the IAIA. I was really amazed at the level of craftsmanship, and I just thought, *Well, maybe this is a possibility. Maybe I could actually make a living doing this.* It was an aha moment: Here's a group of artists that showed it was obtainable to get to that level. And they all went to the same school that I was going to; maybe I could aspire to be something like this.

ON CHOOSING A MEDIUM

I was trying to find my own authentic style, trying to find something that meant something to me. I mixed sand in with the paint. I built things. I cut the canvas in different shapes. I worked in oils. I worked in acrylic. I worked in encaustic. I was exploring the possibilities: What is the medium that I like the best? But I was always a painter. I just loved color, and I loved the immediacy of it. And it dried quickly. I could finish something in a day.

ON GETTING ABSTRACT

I was working a lot with Native American iconography. I really wanted to explore: What is it that defines Native people, cultures and our own respective tribal origins? And it's our belief system. So I was really looking at the spiritual elements of what it is to believe in ancestral spirits and to honor seasons. And the idea that there are different spiritual realms we co-exist with, and trying to figure out how to paint that. In the end, I realized it was too literal. I moved away from that and into the abstractions of things. That was much more enticing to me.

"

THE WORK THAT I'M ENGAGED IN NOW RETAINS THE REAL CORE OF WHAT HAS ALWAYS DRIVEN ME AS A PAINTER, AND THAT IS RHYTHMS. WHAT ARE THE RHYTHMS OF NATURE?

ON LANDSCAPES

I ended up getting married, moving to Taos, raising two kids. That process, and living in this really beautiful environment with mountains and rivers and canyons—all of it became a whole new inspiration. It was like, here's the spiritual in nature. So I started looking at how I could capture that and identify it as my own interpretation of my vernacular. Where do I come from? Where am I living, and what am I seeing and experiencing? And I spent a lot of time outside. I was seeing mountains and clouds and weather, and I was like, *Wow, how do I paint this? How do I capture this in some way?* And I said, *Well, just look at it, experience it, feel it.* And then in the studio, I would just try to get it down as quickly as I could. Often I was working from just a snapshot or a memory of what was transpiring in the clouds. So that became part of a whole new way of seeing the spiritual in my surroundings. There were patterns and rhythms and the connection between earth and sky, clouds, formation, movements.

ON THE WORK'S EVOLUTION

Sometimes when you get good at something, it becomes almost formulaic. And then it's not as inspiring. It doesn't have the same gravitas as it did in the beginning. So I ended up working on these big abstract drawings, which were done on paper and then mounted on canvas. The work that I'm engaged in now is about merging some of those things, but retaining the real core of what has always driven me as a painter, and that is rhythms. What are the rhythms of nature?

ON INSPIRATION

I'm somewhat of a Kerouac man. For me, the journey is part of the art, and you don't really have a story to tell unless you take that journey. Gathering information, painting landscapes, making jewelry, black-and-white drawings, Navajo deities—all of it is part of those life experiences. All of my experiences have made a world that's really just a beautiful experience. If I hadn't become a painter, then maybe I should have been a writer, because then I could describe what this feels like. What is this experience? We all get a different call to do something in our life, and mine was to be an artist and be a painter.

PAINTING THE LAND

Capturing moments of the desert's forever-evolving color and light

TONY ABEYTA, *New Mexico Village - Dancing Skies,* oil on canvas, 2018

Laurie Anne Gonzalez works out of her home studio in Phoenix [with help from her pup, Hazel].

▷ **LAURIE ANNE GONZALEZ**
Pink Desert
Acrylic on canvas

DOUG WEST
Chimayo Arroyo
Oil on canvas
2016

Doug West has been capturing the lands and skies of New Mexico in bold color for more than three decades.

I come from a long lineage of women who work in clay. My grandmother was a potter. My mother was a potter. It was my mother who gave me my first ball of clay, at the ripe age of three or four years old. So I was playing around with the clay very early on. I had a pretty severe speech impediment, which made it hard for me to form words. I was struggling with communication, and I quickly found that if I sculpted, if I coiled a little figurine that showed what I was going through and gave it to my mother, it was a really good way of telling her what was going on with me. I think my style emerged from this need for communication. Being human, I was creating human figures, and they got very expressive because I needed their expressions to talk for me. I got good at it because I continued to use it and still use it for the same reasons, even though now I can talk. I find that expressing things through these human figures and the forms of human expression captures stuff that is sometimes hard to put in words. But people understand it intuitively because of our innate language of feelings. We understand when somebody's happy, when somebody's hurting, when somebody's excited. We understand that in our bodies.

Roxanne Swentzell

Sculptor, Permaculturist

Sydney Brink, Courtesy Palace of the Governor's Photo Archives [NMHM DCA], HP.2014.14.711.

FRITZ SCHOLDER
Indian Image
Acrylic on canvas
1972

*Scholder's work
is considered
revolutionary for the
way it challenged
stereotypes of Native
Americans and
expectations of Native
American art.*

JAUNE QUICK-TO-SEE SMITH
Untitled (Prairie)
Pastel and charcoal on paper
2016

"My work has layered meanings, so you can see many different levels within one single work. I like to bring the viewer in with a seductive texture, a beautiful drawing, [and] then let them have one of the messages."

Jaune Quick-to-See Smith
Artist

Nancy Odegaard

During her long career, retired art conservator Nancy Odegaard tapped into a wide range of interests, boldly embracing the intermingling of disciplines that first drew her to the field.

Over her nearly four decades at the Arizona State Museum on the campus of the University of Arizona in Tucson, Nancy Odegaard's titles were many: conservator, professor, researcher, author, head of preservation, and director of the museum's conservation laboratory. During Odegaard's tenure, the lab conducted groundbreaking research that helped shape the evolving, interdisciplinary field of object conservation through chemistry, engineering, anthropology and more. She retired in 2021.

ON HANDMADE THINGS

I always loved museums. I really loved working with things, handmade things especially. When I was younger, I always wanted to do art things, but I wanted to know more about how it was done. How'd they do that? How do you make that? And how did it come out that way? That led to my interest in archaeology: You're looking at clues, and then you're looking at deterioration. I realized that these things went hand in hand. How something was made also tells you how it's deteriorating, and you can actually draw some connections. In my work, I had a huge platform to look at the old and the new, the damaged and the pristine and the innovative. I've just really enjoyed, tremendously, the ability to look really closely at what people make.

ON MERGING ART AND SCIENCE

In college, I thought of going into something like biology, the sciences, which I enjoyed a lot. But I took an elective art history class and just said, "Well, this is what I really like." Through conservation, I ended up marrying those interests all the way through. What I realized over time, in working with other types of museum professionals—curators, registrars, directors and so on—was that I really liked the interface of the science and the art.

ON RAW MATERIALS

Living in Tucson, I have a close connection to the environment and the raw materials. I can go hiking and see all kinds of things that I know can be made into objects and artwork, and recognize where people may have harvested or sought those materials. One example is the yucca plant. I can see different species and know, *Ah, that one's really good for basketry. That one's really good for cordage. That one makes a good adhesive. This one makes good soap.* I enjoy that such amazing, beautiful things are just there.

ON KNOWING WHAT TO FIX

With a basket, a piece of pottery, you need to understand how it's made. And then when something is damaged, you do what you can to allow it to be stable and not deteriorate further. But you don't add yourself. You have to address whatever is the problem. Sometimes that's putting something back together because it's broken. But sometimes it's corrosion or a color change or a stain—I have to be very careful with anything I remove, because it may be unsightly to a curator, but it may actually be totally related to the object's original use. We have to make some tough decisions along the way. Deciphering what's important and how far to clean, how far to change, is really critical.

"

I CAN APPRECIATE TECHNOLOGY, BUT SEEING THE ROLE OF THE HUMAN IN WHAT'S BEING MADE IS PARTICULARLY JOYFUL FOR ME.

ON READING A PIECE'S HISTORY

To deal with the museum's 20,000 pots was about a 10-year project, and to deal with about 35,000 pieces of fiber, basketry and textile fiber was another 10 years. That's a lot of material to locate, upgrade, document, rehouse. By the time you've looked at many thousands of pieces, you have a sense. You can read the situation. If something was excavated many, many decades ago, I'm looking at: How was it washed by the archaeologist in the field and how was it put together? Was that done with any skill? How is the adhesive holding up? I can probably recognize the adhesive; I've seen so many now. And I can probably tell what was damaged from inadvertent accidents during study or research, versus use-wear from some cultural application. I can start to see details that allow me to enhance the story. And that's fun.

ON THE PERSONAL STORIES OBJECTS TELL

We have about 2,000 archaeological sandals. They're stunning, and gosh, they're so personal. You see the size and see that the designs are unique, so it's a whole picture of how somebody lived. You see something that's been used: A favorite tool, a favorite bowl. A favorite outfit, favorite sandals. You see that something was cared for, but worn, and it was kept. Sometimes we see repairs that do not return the object's function. Somebody was keeping it because it was important, probably sentimentally. Most of us have those kinds of things in our own lives, some nice item: *It's broken, but I just like it. I'm still going to keep it, even though I can't use it anymore.* When you see evidence of that, that's actually very special. I can appreciate technology, but seeing the role of the human in what's being made is particularly joyful for me.

ON DECISIONS ABOUT INDIGENOUS MATERIALS

What began as a troubling spot for me, and what pushed me to do doctoral research and work on this subject, was this: What if I'm messing things up? Who's deciding? And now, I think, the relationships are stronger, particularly in North America and particularly in the Southwest. It's not uncommon to work with community members and get their opinion, and to determine together what's the right thing to do. There's just better dialogue, better relationships.

Pueblo Bonito
CHACO CANYON, NM

From a mesa top, sprawling living spaces and ceremonial kivas of Chaco Canyon's biggest great house stretch on and on.

Petroglyph Trail
CHACO CANYON, NM

Chaco Canyon's bounty of rock art includes petroglyphs that may depict celestial events, like the appearance of a supernova, Halley's Comet and a solar eclipse.

▷

Three Rivers
Petroglyph Site
NEAR TULAROSA, NM

More than 21,000 petroglyphs tell their stories across a ridge of basalt above the Three Rivers Valley. This one depicts a bighorn.

"On the daily, we generally use clay vessels to feed ourselves. I grew up in a mud house, so it was my protection. And we grow our food in the earth. Even though I use a lot of metal and a lot of other materials, like paint, I keep going back to clay because of what it reminds me of: the humanity within myself."

Rose B. Simpson
Mixed-Media Artist

GEORGIA O'KEEFFE
Black Mesa Landscape,
New Mexico / Out Back
of Marie's II
Oil on canvas
1930

Ellen Meloy
The Anthropology of Turquoise

"

Of all the things I wondered about on this land, I wondered the hardest about the seduction of certain geographies that feel like home—not by story or blood but merely by their forms and colors. How our perceptions are our only internal map of the world, how there are places that claim you and places that warn you away. How you can fall in love with the light.

2

The daily movements, techniques and grace that bring forth art from skilled hands

Practice

Ed Sandoval, pictured in his Taos gallery, has a deep reverence for the scenes of New Mexico, dating back to his own childhood.

Potter Kate Brown works the clay at her studio in New Mexico's Mimbres Valley.

▷

Blacksmith Nick Barton hand-forges functional items such as knives and frying pans in his studio in Silver City, New Mexico.

Keri Ataumbi

Native imagery, old European styles, engaging with the world through travel: the inspirations behind Keri Ataumbi's jewelry are as varied as the designs themselves.

Kiowa jeweler Keri Ataumbi grew up on the Wind River Reservation in Wyoming and has lived in Santa Fe for more than three decades. Ataumbi's innovative handmade jewelry is wearable art that combines Native and non-Native cultural aesthetics. In 2015, Keri and her sister, the beadworker Teri Greeves, were honored as Living Treasures by the Museum of Indian Arts and Culture in Santa Fe.

ON CROSS-CULTURAL VALUE SYSTEMS

In my work, I take things that are valuable to us as Native people, like porcupine hair, porcupine quills, tanned buckskin and shells—things that are not considered valuable in the contemporary jewelry world. There are a couple different reasons why all of this is valuable to us. One is the environment it comes from, like the clean water that's required for that porcupine to live. The other is the actual handiwork that goes into it: A tremendous amount of time and consideration and symbology is wrapped up within the work. I'm interested in taking that aspect of the aesthetic in which I was raised and combining it with things that are valuable in the jewelry world: high-carat gold, diamonds, rubies, emeralds—some of which is valuable because of its rarity, and some of which is valuable because man said it was.

ON GETTING INTO JEWELRY

After I finished my bachelor's degree at the College of Santa Fe, I started taking classes at the community college because I was missing the structure of the classroom. I took a jewelry class, and it was love at first sight. The second I was in that jewelry lab, there were bells and whistles going off inside of me, and it was all I could think about. And I'm still kind of like that.

ON TRAVELING

The Kiowa word: *hope-khoam* means "loves to go" or "likes to travel." [Kiowa is not a written language. The closest is the linguistic version, referred to as the Mackenzie version, but this spelling is phonetic.] With that is the feeling of "get up and go"—you just travel; I think that's a specific Kiowa personality. Travel is really important to me. My mom instilled that in us. She had a trading post, and when I was 17, she sold a big piece and sent my sister and me to Kenya. It was the first time I was ever out of this country, and I knew: *I have to make sure that I do this as often as I possibly can throughout my entire life, to get outside of my comfort zone.* How my schedule generally runs is, I have intense periods of work in the studio—I pretty much walk my dog, go to the gym, go to the grocery store, and work—and then I'll flip to traveling, which is a different way of being engaged in the world. We all tend to get in our groove of however we're working, living or seeing the world. When you travel, you are forced to take those blinders off and fully engage with the landscape around you.

ON CONTINUING TO LEARN

It's a practice of mine, and I always tell my students this, to always take at least one class a year. I make sure that I have enrolled in some class every year, because you learn different things from different people. I have a drawing instructor, and I take jewelry workshops all the time—different types of stone setting, and there's a kajillion different types of tools in jewelry making. So you can take a class that specifically talks about a specific tool and determine whether you want to buy that tool or not. I'm at the place where I'm buying tools like a laser welder—a significant tool—not just a hammer.

"
THE SECOND I WAS IN THAT JEWELRY LAB, THERE WERE BELLS AND WHISTLES GOING OFF INSIDE OF ME, AND IT WAS ALL I COULD THINK ABOUT.

Courtesy of Keri Ataumbi

ON CONNECTION TO THE LAND

The Cerrillos Hills behind my house have always had turquoise in them. We were on this big trade route—if you think about the geography of Turtle Island, that Southwest area is kind of the hub. You can see where the mines are, and they've all basically been filled in. There's a few active mines, but they're not *really* active; it's just someone with a mining claim who's out there looking for a little bit of turquoise. But you can see the different levels: where the natives were mining, then the Spaniards coming in, and then Anglos, each digging deeper. I just have an affinity for that land. I go out there every day and walk 3 to 5 miles. I work at home, and if I get into a rut or I'm getting frustrated, that is the answer. It has, to this day, never failed to help me shift out of that.

ON MAKING INTAGLIO RINGS

They're hand carved—generally in quartz crystal, but sometimes lapis, and sometimes a more expensive stone like aquamarine—and then I set them in silver or gold. My original intaglios were clearly Native imagery, a lance or a golden arrow or a pot or a native warrior or a feather. But now I'm doing a lot of animals, bears and buffalo and whatever I decide to do. The idea is that it's like your signet ring or your power ring. If you're in a meeting, you can look down at it and have that power of that snake or whatever it is on your finger. They're really fun.

I have some Italian heritage, and I love old European styles. And at this point, we're so mixed in our cultures. If you look at Kiowa beadwork, for example, you can see changes the minute that soldiers arrived. The patterns start changing into fleurs de lis and different, more European shapes. Yet they still read very Kiowa. That's just artists interpreting the world around them. The intaglio are like that for me.

Apache artist Allan Houser [with his 1987 sculpture Anasazi] *worked for many years from his family compound south of Santa Fe,* 1991.

Allan Houser Inc., courtesy of the Allan Houser Foundation Archives

"God and the Great Spirit
gave me [hands] that work. ...
God gave me that hand,
but not for myself, for
all my people."

Maria Montoya Martinez

**MARIA MARTINEZ AND
JULIAN MARTINEZ**
Black Feather Pot
Ceramic
Ca. 1945-1960

**MARIA MARTINEZ AND
SANTANA MARTINEZ**
Black Feather Plate
Ceramic
Ca. 1945-1960

Rich veins of turquoise run through the Cerrillos Hills. In 1889, Tiffany & Company bought up mines whose turquoise matched the company's signature green-blue.

DINÉ WEAVERS

A history-steeped textile tradition evolving with the generations

Kevin Aspaas lives near
Shiprock, a peak sacred to
the Diné (Navajo) people.

To dye wool, Venancio Aragon uses natural materials like indigo alongside synthetic dyes.

A Diné woman weaves
at the Gallup Ceremonial
Celebration, 1948.

Venancio Aragon gathers
traditional materials for
his natural dyes.

"To find things that are authentic, it might take a little bit of patience and searching. But those things are out there, and Santa Fe is that kind of place. There are so many layers to Santa Fe— you have to dig a little below the surface and be patient enough to look and take your time."

Jed Foutz
Owner, Shiprock Santa Fe

My grandmother's people, who are my mother's people, who are my people, are people of the land. Indigenous people. • It's said that our Diné men would cut the heels off their boots to walk more softly upon the earth. • It's said that the Spider Woman taught us to weave, that Talking God told us the sheep were placed for us. To watch for them. • We are like seeds. Some of us removed from the land Creator gave us. Some of us still rooted. But we carry the memory of our creation stories in our DNA. We wear that memory in our hair, upon our chests, on our feet. We wear that memory into the wildness, and into urban jungles built on ancestors' bones. • One could argue that until we were taught English, "fashion" didn't exist for us. Fashion carries a legacy of taking, of individualism and greed. The history of silk, cotton, indigo and whalebone alone shows the pain, both to the environment and human beings, for which fashion set the stage. • In the Indigenous world, clothing was/is created out of an inherent relationship with the land and one another. Some practices were taught to us by Creator, or different holy people, and others were learned by listening to the animals, plants and water. Clothing, adornment, regalia were/are symbolic, sacred, a poetry of sustainability and kinship. An ongoing narrative of survival. • Diné weavers like Roy Kady and Naiomi Glasses have long used sheep to maintain their land in the Southwest. "Spider Man and Spider Woman were the ones that introduced weaving in the underworld," says Kady. "The sheep are a life giver in so many ways; they teach us survival skills. They provide us with clothing, they maintain the land, and there are ceremonies that are structured around the sheep." • Inspired by her kinship to nature, award-winning Taos Pueblo designer Patricia Michaels uses natural dyes, such as algae pigments, to hand-paint organic fabrics with abstract images from nature, inviting wearers into the unique world of Northern New Mexico and Taos Pueblo, her ancestral homeland. • Indigenous people are nothing if not adaptable. Resilient. We are a people that laughs easily and creates easily, because both are reminders that we are alive. • As we break into new worlds, the ideas and lifeways that we have always practiced are assigned names. Names like "fashion." • When the gatekeepers told us we were making fashion, fashion changed forever. It became something that could contain multiple perspectives, multiple kinships, multiple spaces in time. It opened the door to walking more softly upon the earth. Hundreds if not thousands of Indigenous people in North America alone are creating and selling fashion and adornment to the outside world, using practices that predate colonialism. These practices—remembered, passed down or relearned—are all rooted in the stewardship of our land, the land Creator gave us to protect and sustain. To die for. • Every English word is foreign in our mouths, even when it is the only language we speak. So we communicate in other ways. Indigenous makers are speaking in a language given to them by their Creator, by listening to the animals and plants. By listening to the water. By listening to one another. Some of this language is ancient. Some of it is still being born.

Dispatch: WEARING THE LAND

BY UNGELBAH DÁVILA-SHIVERS

The weaving knowledge goes back to when my family first settled in Chimayo in the 1700s. They brought European-style weaving—the European loom is different from the Native loom because it works with a harness that separates the strings. At the time, it was an isolated area, so they wove out of necessity; they raised the sheep and did the wool processing. Around 1900, my grandparents married. My grandfather built the lower portion of the building that we're still in, and he included a little general store. He had a loom set up, and he would weave between customers or when he wasn't farming. With the advent of the automobile, more people started coming around, and he couldn't produce enough himself, so he contracted with other local people. It's pretty much the way we still do it today; most people who weave for us learn through their families. A Chimayo weaving has a dominant background color, and generally there are striped borders toward the ends and geometric designs incorporated in the center. The weavers pick the designs and color combinations; every weaver has their way.

Robert Ortega

Weaving Shop Owner

Saguaro National Park
TUSCON, AZ

Virgil Ortiz

Moving seamlessly from pottery to fashion design to apocalyptic sci-fi storytelling, Virgil Ortiz's revolutionary artwork bends genre and form—and his biggest project is still unfolding.

Born into a family of potters and raised in Cochiti Pueblo, Virgil Ortiz always knew he wanted to be an artist. In addition to pottery, his work ranges from a fashion line to a Cochiti-inspired jewelry collaboration with the Smithsonian to his ongoing multimedia project *Revolt 1680/2180*, in which Pueblo history meets sci-fi.

ON TRADITIONAL POTTERY

"Traditional" means we collect all the materials; they're all from the earth. When I was a kid, the whole family would go on a trip once a year to gather the clay. We'd bring it home, store it in the barn until it got bone-dry, because it comes out of the earth damp, and it's so pure, hence very hard to work with, and sticky. It takes a year to process the clay. The traditional work is the heart and soul of everything that I do. It's the nucleus, and all the other different types of medium orbit around it. I keep that work, the traditional clay, only at Cochiti.

ON STORYTELLERS

Cochiti is known for the making of storytelling figures: a seated woman, or grandmother, or a bear, or animals carrying their kids. Our language isn't written, so these figures were named "storytellers," and it's how we pass down our language. I was taught how to make these types of figures, and also the pots with geometrical designs that incorporate the earth's elements, like clouds, rain, thunder and all the different materials, like the wild spinach we use to make the black paint on our pottery.

ON FINDING A STYLE

When I was 13 to 15, I started making standing figures and painting them with more of a fashion sense. One of the dealers who visited the pueblo on buying trips noticed that my pieces were going outside of the box. He asked my parents, "Who's teaching this kid how to make these figures and how he's painted them?" My parents told him I was just experimenting. He invited my parents and me to his showroom in Albuquerque. It turned out he had the largest collection of historic Pueblo pottery from the 1800s. And all of my experimental pottery and figures looked exactly like them without having ever seen them before. That connection and influence that came from somewhere flipped my parents—and me—out. They took me outside and told me, "We didn't teach you any of this, and you can see the clay is talking to you and through you. So remember this day from now on."

ON HOW IDEAS ARRIVE

I call myself a conduit. I don't feel it's my talent; it's just lent to me for a while, while I'm here on this earth. So I better do something good with it. If I'm influenced by something, or if I get a message while I'm asleep, when I wake up, I know exactly what I'm supposed to create. I try to sketch ideas in clay, but the clay makes itself, basically. No matter how much you design it, it changes. It has a mind of its own. Whether it be clothing, pattern-making or whatever designs I put on the clay, it just feeds itself. It flows and I don't question it, because one medium leads to the next.

"I TRY TO SKETCH IDEAS IN CLAY, BUT THE CLAY MAKES ITSELF, BASICALLY.

ON GOING BEYOND CLAY

When I was in high school and I couldn't afford the clothes I'd seen in magazines, that sparked me to try to make my own clothes. I learned how to sew from my mother and my sisters. Right away, I started creating with leather and vinyl latex. After I did that, I found out that those are the hardest materials to work with. Now I can make any kind of clothing that I've seen or that I want. It developed into costuming, and now a full line of ready-to-wear—and high-end leather handbags, accessories, cuffs, everything like that.

ON *REVOLT 1680/2180*

I wanted to tell the story of the 1680 Pueblo Revolt happening simultaneously in two different time dimensions, 2180 and 1680. Jumping back and forth, teleporting and time jumping. That's where the Indigenous futurism came into play. I developed 19 groups of characters that represent the 19 pueblos that are still left in New Mexico today. Creating all these characters allowed me to bring in the sci-fi storytelling aspect, which I loved as a kid. I was highly impacted by the *Star Wars* movies. I'd seen the original when I was six or seven years old, and it stuck with me. I knew all the characters—where they came from, what they did, how they dressed, what kind of ships they drove, the languages, the costuming.

ON THE BLIND ARCHER

The Blind Archer is the main character. The original person who devised the Pueblo Revolt, from Ohkay Owingeh Pueblo just north of Santa Fe, was named Po'pay. I wanted to give Po'pay a sidekick, and behind every man, there's a smarter woman. Just watching how my mom and aunts, sisters, nieces were all the powerhouse behind what we do in this world, I wanted to pay attention to women's empowerment and give the kids a woman superhero.

ON PURPOSE

I feel I'm here on earth to make sure that Cochiti pottery, using traditional methods and materials, doesn't die out as an art form, because all of our masters are passing away. The second part of why I feel I'm here on this earth is to educate the world about the 1680 Pueblo Revolt. Most people don't know of that historic moment, even though it was America's first revolution. I want to educate using art. The more art I make about it, the more it brings attention to it so we don't repeat it.

Maynard Dixon

"

As to my technique, it is no accident, and is developed to meet my needs. My "feeling" is toward the thing I do, and austerity and clear definition are the dominating character of the arid lands I work in.

3

Masterpieces past and present, from gallery walls to bustling summer markets

Works

BEATIEN YAZZ
Bison at Bay
Watercolor
Undated

*Clayton Porter's "Bronc
Riders" pack painstaking
detail into minute spaces
surrounded by blankness.*

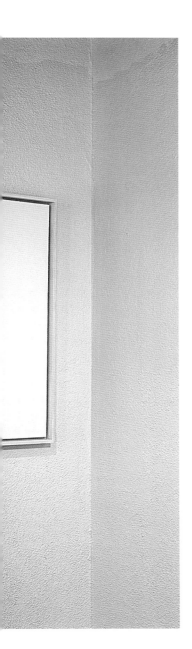

The best art moments are the ones that catch you by surprise. The way the Brutalist concrete walls at Tucson MOCA, for instance, made a perfect backdrop to the huge paintings in Rosson Crow's 2018 *Westification* show, highlighting their power to at once celebrate and subvert. It had to do with the subject matter: the many-armed saguaros, scores of them, along with prickly pear and organ pipe. Then, the close framing, everything crowded into the foreground, a contrast to the broad-skied vistas we expect from Southwestern paintings. Also, the colors—flashes of cherry red, smears of radioactive pink—and how, looking closer, I noticed plant pots, beer cans, cardboard smiley faces. Shopping bags, oil drums, chain-link fences, all tucked among the cacti. Were we indoors or out? In nature or a backlot or a simulation? Was this beauty or toxicity? And—in today's world—could any of this really be parsed? • These tensions, wielded by a new generation of Southwestern artists, come to mind on the day I visit Clayton Porter at his studio in Santa Fe. In paintings from the region, it is typical for a figure on horseback to take up only a small part of the scene. Picture it: the pair viewed from afar, cresting a hill or fording a stream, forming a subtle point of action in the much grander landscape. The figures Porter calls his "Bronc Riders" are small as well. In his studio hangs a 4-foot-square panel on which he has been drawing—slowly, painstakingly, with many pauses to sharpen his pencil—a 2-inch-wide image of a rodeo cowboy on a bucking horse. What is most striking, however, is that the surrounding landscape has gone missing. There is no epic sweep of great sky here, nor will there be. In its place is an airless white void. • This horse-and-rider image is organic to Porter's own life, born of formative years spent with his roping-enthusiast father, and he unofficially groups them under the moniker "Latigo," after the leather strap used to tie things to a saddle. But these cowboys and cowgirls are displaced—apart from context, outside of time and story and landscape. And in this way, Porter, like Crow with her saguaros, twists a classic trope to both celebrate and cleverly undercut our expectations. His is a void that feels like a critique, like a mirror, reflecting our own projections back at us. It is the flatness of mythos, of stereotype, of centuries' worth of fantasies foisted onto this region, which even now is still sometimes taken for a blank slate. • Yet what makes these pieces so tricky and compelling, to me, is the way the void oddly elevates the horse and rider. It is gripping, even poignant, how these men and women cling to their mounts, giving in to neither the absence that engulfs them nor the small chaos that consumes their attention. It conjures the complicated legacies of Anglo-American settlement and heritage [Crow's and mine and part of Porter's] and questions about what we might owe this place now. Because, as Porter points out, the moment's end—that feared, anticipated fall— is not just likely but inevitable.

Dispatch: VARIATIONS ON A THEME

ARTURO CHAVEZ
Place Where They
Threw the Rocks Down
Oil on canvas
2021

Cody Hartley

Being the director of Santa
Fe's Georgia O'Keeffe
Museum means celebrating
the artist's work, grappling
with her complicated legacy
and always thinking about
the local community.

Cody Hartley has worked at the Georgia O'Keeffe Museum in Santa Fe, where he is now the director, since 2013. His love of the New Mexico art world goes way back, though he also spent time at Boston's Museum of Fine Arts, the Sterling and Francine Clark Art Institute in Williamstown, Massachusetts, and the Santa Barbara Museum of Art along the way.

ON FAMILY TIES TO NEW MEXICO

My grandparents spent a lot of time earlier in their lives in New Mexico. My grandmother worked at Los Alamos. After World War II, my grandfather came back and enrolled in the MFA program at the University of New Mexico. They eventually moved to Colorado, where they raised my mother, but they kept coming back every summer to visit friends. So my mother also spent a lot of her childhood in New Mexico. And she was in a gallery in Taos when she decided that she was going to be an artist when she grew up.

ON BEING DRAWN THERE

I never had a chance to actually visit New Mexico until I was in my late teens, when I spent a spring break in Taos and Santa Fe. I fell in love, thought it was amazing, and also found it really unexpected—and a little confusing. The wealth of art, the number of museums, galleries, the cultural richness of this city just really surprised me and defied my understanding. Even in the '90s, when I first started visiting, Santa Fe was still relatively hard to get to. It's not on a major pathway. There's not a major airport. How could it have so much culture? And so I got the bug.

ON ART RESEARCH

I eventually decided that I really wanted to try to answer for myself: Why was Santa Fe such a cultural destination? My dissertation was an attempt to answer that question. I looked at the creation of the museum system, the early patronage of Indian arts, artists from the East Coast moving to Santa Fe and setting up shop. I was trying to figure out how Santa Fe became so prominent and the publicizing mechanisms that attracted people to live and work in the city.

ON MOVING TO SANTA FE

In 2005, I thought, *All right, I've answered my questions about New Mexico. I'm moving to the East Coast; I've got it out of my system.* Of course, I did not have it out of my system. In 2012, the O'Keeffe Museum called and invited me to take a position. And once I came back, I fell in love all over again. After I moved here, my mother started telling me those stories about my grandparents, and I thought, *Wow, it's like the pathway was always there.* I could only see it looking behind me, but I was always on a pathway taking me back to New Mexico.

ON O'KEEFFE'S WORK AND LIFE

Her artwork is the core of what we do, but her life is so fascinating. We can tell that story through the material culture, the objects that she left: The rocks, shells and bones she collected. The paint materials, the clothing, the furnishing, the archival documents. We're building a new facility that will allow us to dramatically expand the amount of work we can show from the rest of our collections, outside of the fine arts paintings. It'll really expand the stories we can tell.

"
O'KEEFFE'S ARTWORK IS THE CORE OF WHAT WE DO, BUT HER LIFE IS SO FASCINATING.

ON ROOTEDNESS IN NEW MEXICO

One could have built a Georgia O'Keeffe museum in New York, or in her birthplace of Wisconsin, or other places where she lived and worked. So it matters that we are in Santa Fe. It matters that we're in New Mexico, because this place was so important in her own personal growth and development. It's where she rebuilt her creativity, rejuvenated herself. It inspired decades of fresh, creative artwork. So to connect to the place and understand its importance is a critical responsibility for us. I love our visitors, and we always want to be able to satisfy their curiosity to understand more about her life and to see her artwork. But I also feel a powerful need to support our communities, to support the wellbeing of our neighbors throughout the town of Santa Fe and throughout the broader region.

ON O'KEEFFE'S IMPACT ON NEW MEXICO

She was a very generous individual. She helped her neighbors. She tried to do right by the community. But we also have an obligation, in this day and age, to think about some of the unintended consequences. She is easily the most well-known artist associated with New Mexico, so she drives visibility and visitation in many ways. At the same time, that fame can obliterate a lot of other activities, other great artists in the area. What we are really trying to understand is: How do we think through the story of Georgia O'Keeffe's life and the decades after her death? What are the positive benefits of that visibility, of tourism? And what are the risks? What are the dangers?

ON UNINTENDED CONSEQUENCES

While I don't think it was intentional on her part—she probably couldn't even have imagined or been aware of it—it's undeniable that she's kind of the face of gentrification. There's this desire to live the way Georgia O'Keeffe lived in this landscape, which is wonderful—but it is not always without costs. So we're trying to understand the displacement, the degree to which outside wealth has dispossessed our Indigenous and Hispanic neighbors who have called this place home for hundreds, if not thousands, of years. I think it is a moral obligation on our part to recognize these serious repercussions and to focus on how we can instead use the platform we've been given—the visibility and resources we have because of her success—to not just celebrate her own independent spirit, but to bring positive impact to the people who live on the land and in the communities that inspired her originally.

R.C. GORMAN
Three Women
Edition 103-120
Lithograph
1977

When artist R.C. Gorman opened the Navajo Gallery in Taos in 1968, it was the first Indigenous-owned gallery in the country.

Fritz Scholder
Leonardo Vol. 6, No. 2 [Spring 1973]

"

My work startled many people because I, part-Indian, treated the Indian differently, not as the "noble savage" endlessly portrayed by White painters, and also because my technique was non-Indian (my work was not flat and decorative). I felt it to be a compliment when I was told that I had destroyed the traditional style of Indian art, for I was doing what I thought had to be done.

INTERVIEW:

Helen R. Lucero

Dr. Helen R. Lucero
devoted her career to
teaching the public about
Hispanic arts—and
striving to make the field
more accessible to those
who came after her.

One of the first female Hispanic curators in the United States, Helen worked at many museums across her career, including the Museum of International Folk Art in Santa Fe, the National Hispanic Cultural Center in Albuquerque and the Smithsonian American Art Museum in Washington, D.C. She is also the co-author, with Suzanne Baizerman, of *Chimayó Weaving: The Transformation of a Tradition*. She retired in 2006.

ON SEEING POSSIBILITIES

I grew up in this tiny village called Vadito in Northern New Mexico, on the high road to Taos. I was in the middle of all those *santos* and *retablos* that eventually became what I studied at the university and in my museum positions, but I didn't think of them as art. At age 12 or 13, I started visiting my aunt and uncle in Las Vegas, New Mexico, which was a huge, different thing, because I grew up with no running water, no electricity, no paved roads, none of that. So Las Vegas was a big city for me. It had all of that and more, including a very grainy black-and-white television. That opened my eyes to all kinds of possibilities. And at 15, I came with my sister to Albuquerque. We rented an apartment and had a marvelous time as waitresses in the big city. That started the whole thing of seeing what else was possible in the world.

ON LEARNING ART TO CURATE ART

I took an art course, I think, every semester that I ever went to school. So in the end, when I did get the museum positions, I knew about printmaking, I knew about ceramics, I knew about jewelry. I knew about all these different art forms in terms of the process, which was very important, I felt, to really understand and be able to speak about it knowledgeably. And I continued doing my own artwork once I retired. My very last exhibit was of my own work. After that, I thought, *Okay, I finished. I've done it.*

ON THE REVIVAL OF TRADITIONAL ART FORMS

The *bultos* and the *retablos* were the types of artwork that you would find in the churches or the *moradas* [the chapter houses for the lay *penitentes*, the brothers]. Bultos in the round are sculptural, and the retablos are the flat ones. These were produced before the mills came in, so the wood is hand-etched. Later, you have works being produced on flat boards out of milled lumber. But a lot of the current-day *santeros* have gone back to producing similar kinds of work in terms of the materials.

The tin work originated from cans of goods, like lard and so on, that came in tin—which then got recycled and made into frames, or what are called *nichos*, places to put religious images or flowers or things. The tin work was dominated by one family, the Romeros. Emilio and Senaida Romero were very active in that. Their sons and daughters have almost all continued doing it. A lot of them have passed on now, but they were able to teach the art form to many of their descendants. Colcha embroidery was another form that was revived. Then you have the weaving, which is the one that I knew best from my research—when the Spanish first arrived here, they brought the knowledge of how to produce these beautiful weavings. The Ortegas and the Trujillos in Chimayó have had shops where they have hired people as a cottage industry for years and years. That's another art form that continues to this day.

> # MY VERY LAST EXHIBIT WAS OF MY OWN WORK. AFTER THAT, I THOUGHT, OKAY, I FINISHED. I'VE DONE IT.

ON DISCRIMINATION IN THE ART WORLD

When I came back to New Mexico after I had worked at the Museum of Modern Art and the Dallas Museum—yes, one was as a membership secretary, the other as a receptionist, but I had been in both of those museums—I couldn't even get an interview for a secretarial job. They just were not going to give me a chance. So I continued going to school, figuring, *Well, maybe when I get my master's*—and then a bunch of rejections. I was about halfway through my PhD dissertation when I applied for a job at the Museum of International Folk Art. I was not really qualified for the job: curator of Latin American arts, meaning art from El Salvador and Mexico and everywhere else south. I didn't have that kind of a background. But having been working on my dissertation on Hispanic weaving and being from Northern New Mexico and knowing so many of the artists, when I interviewed for the job, the director kept asking me questions about New Mexican arts. They created a half-time position for me because they were going to open the first Hispanic heritage wing in Santa Fe. This was in 1984. I was the first Hispanic there in a position, other than the guards or the maintenance crew and one or two Hispanic secretaries. It was a constant battle for me to get things done in a way that was respectful and that I felt was important to our culture.

ON CHANGES IN THE INDUSTRY

After I retired in 2006, I began to see the changes, like with Tey Marianna Nunn, who took over the position I had had at the National Hispanic Cultural Center. And today, I see that there are quite a few more Hispanic curators, especially young women. Recently, I was looking through some files, and I saw that, at one point, I wrote an article called "The Challenges of Being a Hispanic Curator." All the way back in the '80s, I was thinking about the challenges.

Hasburg

ANDREW MICHAEL
DASBURG
*Road to Lamy,
New Mexico*
Oil on canvas
1923

113

"Nampeyo set out first to show the process of coiling a vessel. The even 'ropes' of clay were rolled out from her smooth palms in a marvelous way, and efforts to rival excited a smile from the family sitting around as interested spectators."

Walter Hough
The Hopi Indians, 1915

Edward S. Curtis, Image History Collection / Alamy Stock Photo.

Tewa Hopi potter Nampeyo
sits on a mat, painting designs
on her pottery, ca. 1900.

THE
MARKETS

Come summer, Santa Fe fills with vibrant, authentic artworks of all kinds

Crowds fill Santa Fe's Lincoln
Avenue to browse the annual
Indian Market, the largest
Native American art market
in the world, 1988.

Mary Rose Toya [Jemez Pueblo] displays pottery at Indian Market, 1988.

The Sunday Procession emerges from St. Francis Basilica and continues through the plaza during Santa Fe's Spanish Market.

Frank L. Garcia
displays a table full of
colorful bultos, retablos
and hide paintings.

My grandfather owned and operated what was first called Navajo Hopi Indian Store, and then later rebranded Navajo Hopi Trading Post. He purchased the business in the mid-1930s. For 35-plus years, he traded and dealt with some of the luminaries of Southwestern art, specifically Native art. When my grandfather was selling pottery made by Hopi artists in his gallery, the people who bought it referred to it as "Indian crafts." It's always been art, but the way the audience viewed it and understood it has changed. Today, no one refers to the work of Susan Folwell—an incredible Santa Clara ceramic artist—as "crafts"; it's fine art. Or take the work of D.Y. Begay, a Navajo weaver: Her textiles are poetry; they are music. They're transcendent. There is this sculptural quality to them because of the texture and undulations. Her work is incredible, and again, no one's referring to it as crafts. Nobody today goes into a gallery like Shiprock in Santa Fe and says, "Hi, I want to see the Indian crafts." It's world-class jewelry, world-class textiles, world-class everything. The fine arts, as they had traditionally been defined, were painting and printmaking and sculpture. Southwest art has always challenged those structures.

Scott Hale

Art Appraiser

JAUNE QUICK-TO-SEE SMITH
Untitled (Wallowa Waterhole)
Pastel and graphite on paper
1979

FRITZ SCHOLDER
Artist at Forty as a Buffalo
Color lithograph on paper
1977

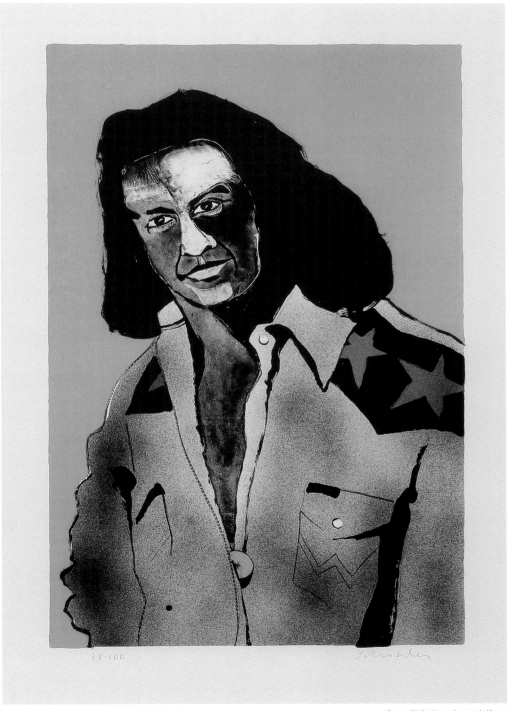

38·100

Maria Martinez's world-renowned pottery was a communal effort: She and members of her family worked closely together at San Ildefonso Pueblo.

Museums

ALBUQUERQUE MUSEUM
Exhibitions explore art, history and culture in the Southwest. A cornerstone of the local cultural community. *Albuquerque*

INDIAN PUEBLO CULTURAL CENTER Museum, galleries, library and more provide a starting point for learning about the past and present of New Mexico's 19 Pueblos. *Albuquerque*

NATIONAL HISPANIC CULTURAL CENTER Preserving Hispanic culture and art through exhibitions and events. The center includes an art museum, theaters and genealogy center. *Albuquerque*

MILLICENT ROGERS MUSEUM
Built upon the socialite's own collections of jewelry, weavings and other art. Rogers' turquoise and silver jewelry collection is on permanent display. *El Prado*

GEORGIA O'KEEFFE MUSEUM
Rotating exhibitions showcase the artist's work and life, from paintings and sketches to rocks and paint pigments. *Sante Fe*

IAIA MUSEUM OF CONTEMPORARY NATIVE ARTS The only institution in the country fully dedicated to sharing the work of contemporary Native artists. *Sante Fe*

MUSEUM OF INDIAN ARTS & CULTURE Telling the stories through culture and art of the peoples of the Southwest, from prehistory to the present day. *Sante Fe*

MUSEUM OF INTERNATIONAL FOLK ART Diverse collections include more than 130,000 examples of folk and traditional arts. Working to expand the understanding of folk art and cultural identity. *Sante Fe*

WHEELWRIGHT MUSEUM OF THE AMERICAN INDIAN Exhibitions often highlight underappreciated art genres. Home to the world's most comprehensive collection of Navajo and Pueblo jewelry. *Sante Fe*

HARWOOD MUSEUM OF ART
Focuses on art from Northern New Mexico, both historic and contemporary, including a gallery devoted to Agnes Martin. *Taos*

AMERIND MUSEUM Dedicated to preserving and interpreting Native American cultures and histories. *Dragoon*

MUSEUM OF NORTHERN ARIZONA Regional learning center celebrating the natural and cultural heritage of the Colorado Plateau. *Flagstaff*

HEARD MUSEUM Telling American Indian stories in close collaboration with artists and tribal communities. *Phoenix*

PHOENIX ART MUSEUM
Biggest visual art museum in the Southwest. Wide-ranging collection covers artworks from across the globe. *Phoenix*

ARIZONA STATE MUSEUM
Exhibits on Indigenous histories and cultures draw from the institution's massive anthropological research repository. *Tucson*

NATIONAL MUSEUM OF THE AMERICAN INDIAN Vast collection of Native objects, photographs and media from across the Western Hemisphere. A Smithsonian institution. *Washington, D.C.*

SMITHSONIAN AMERICAN ART MUSEUM Huge American art collection includes works by many noted Southwest artists, including Georgia O'Keeffe. *Washington, D.C.*

AUTRY MUSEUM OF THE AMERICAN WEST Art and cultural materials bringing together the stories of the peoples of the American West. Includes the Southwest Museum of the American Indian Collection. *Los Angeles*

METROPOLITAN MUSEUM OF ART Largest art museum in the Western Hemisphere features historical and contemporary works, including those of many Southwest artists. *New York*

Galleries

ALBUQUERQUE
fourteenfifteen
516 ARTS
Harwood Art Center
Richard Levy
Sanitary Tortilla Factory

SANTE FE
5. Gallery
Obscura
CURRENTS 826
Ellsworth Gallery
FaraHNHeight
form & concept
Foto Forum
Gerald Peters Gallery
Hecho Gallery
Pie Projects
Shiprock Santa Fe
SITE Santa Fe
Smoke the Moon
Title Gallery

TUCSON
American Institute of
 Thoughts and Feelings
Andrew Smith Gallery
DeGrazia
Etherton Gallery
Everybody
MOCA Tucson
Pidgin Palace Arts

ELSEWHERE
Belhaus *Phoenix, AZ*
Georgia O'Keeffe Homes
 Abiquiú, NM
Larsen Gallery *Scottsdale*
MoMAZoZo *Carrizozo, NM*
Roswell Museum *Roswell, NM*
Through the Flower
 Art Space *Belen, NM*

Artist & Photographer Index

68-69
MINESH BACRANIA
Venancio Aragon
Navajo Nation

70
ROBERT H.MARTIN
Navajo weaver
Gallup, NM, 1948

71
MINESH BACRANIA
Venancio Aragon
Navajo Nation

73
KRYSTA JABCZENSKI
Shiprock Santa Fe
Santa Fe, NM

75
GABRIELLA MARKS
Patricia Michaels
Taos Pueblo

78-79
CASSIDY ARAIZA
Saguaro National Park
Tucson, AZ

81
UNGELBAH DÁVILA-SHIVERS
Virgil Ortiz
Sante Fe, NM

84
NEW MEXICO HISTORY MUSEUM
Patrociño Barela
Taos, NM, ca. 1935

85
PATROCIÑO BARELA
Saint George, Carved juniper, ca. 1935-1943

88
MAYNARD DIXON
Sunset Magazine
Lithograph, 1902

89
MAYNARD DIXON
Overland
Lithograph, 1896

90-91
TONY VACCARO
Georgia O'Keeffe
Abiquiú, NM, 1960

94-95
BEATIEN YAZZ
Bison at Bay
Watercolor, undated

96-97
CLAYTON PORTER
Bronc Riders
Graphite on paper
Sante Fe, NM, 2021

98-99
ARTURO CHAVEZ
Place Where They Threw the Rocks Down
Oil on canvas, 2021

104
R.C. GORMAN
Three Women
Lithograph, 1977

105
NEW MEXICO HISTORY MUSEUM
R.C. Gorman
Taos, NM, ca. 1980

112-113
ANDREW MICHAEL DASBURG
Road to Lamy, New Mexico, oil on canvas, 1923

115
EDWARD S. CURTIS
Nampeyo
Hopi Reservation, AZ, Ca. 1900

117
GABRIELLA MARKS
Indian Market
Santa Fe, NM, 2019

118
LARRY BECKNER
Indian Market
Santa Fe, NM, 1988

119
LARRY BECKNER
Mary Rose Toya
Jemez Pueblo, NM
1988

120
CHARLES MANN
Spanish Market
Santa Fe, NM, 2011

121
CHARLES MANN
Spanish Market
Santa Fe, NM, 2011

124
JAUNE QUICK-TO-SEE SMITH
Untitled [Wallowa Waterhole], Pastel and graphite on paper, 1979

125
FRITZ SCHOLDER
Artist at Forty as a Buffalo
Color lithograph on paper, 1977

126-127
ELDRED HARRINGTON
Maria Martinez
San Ildefonso Pueblo, New Mexico, ca. 1930

128-129
JAY HEMPHILL
Sawyers Peak
Gila National Forest, NM